THE BRIGHT SIDE
OF DARKNESS

REFLECTIONS ON SUFFERING

To Rick + Becky,

Thanks for being
such a bright part
of my life!!
Love,
Glenda
Prov. 3:5-6

ISBN: 0-9762014-8-8
978-0-9762014-8-9

Published by L'Edge Press
A ministry of Upside Down Ministries, Inc.
PO Box 2567
Boone, North Carolina

DEDICATION

To My Husband:
Eddie, who encourages and inspires me, and
who makes me want to be what he thinks I am.

To My Children:
Juliann, Jonathan, Sarah Beth
You challenge me in wonderful ways!!

To My Grandchildren:
Anna Legan and Bailey
You are my two precious angels!!

You all light up my life every day like a
fireworks display lights up the sky. My prayer
for each of you is that you would love the Lord
your God with all your heart, mind, and soul,
and that each of your lives would continually
bring glory to God.

SPECIAL THANKS TO:

Mother, for the Godly example you have set for me for these past sixty-four years. Your prayers, support, and encouragement mean so much to me. Thanks for letting me print your poem, *Sir Sorrow.*

Eddie, for giving me the freedom to focus on what God wanted to do in my life. Thanks for letting me print your song, *Safe in The Hollow of His Hand.* I love you!

Geni, Libbi and Rosemari, for being critics, editors, encouragers, and prayer warriors...for helping make it happen! I really appreciate all you did!

Juliann, for your letter, insight, love, and encouragement.

Jeff Hendley, my publisher, for leading me through the process and helping me to accomplish the impossible.

Jonathan and Sarah Beth West, for the use of your peaceful Beech Mountain, NC, home to write this book, and for your suggestions, encouragement, and love.

Glenn and Donna Bailey, for your invaluable help and your heartfelt addition to this book.

Beth W. Hensley and Libbi Hendley, for sincere, truthful, and inspiring additions to this book.

Ken and Jeanne Ballinger, my new friends, for your careful proofreading and corrections.

Thanks to Donna and Beth for their microscopic look at the manuscript and your suggestions and changes.

The members of Christ Baptist Church, for your continued prayers and encouragement. I love you all!

FOREWORD

It is so interesting that I am able to write this letter of introduction on the author. I am the author's daughter, and to be quite honest the supplier of some of her suffering. What is so beautiful about my mom is her ability to trust God and not worry about things. She has taught me so much, but I am most thankful that she taught me to turn my problems over to God. It is amazing just how calming this is for your spirit. This can radiate from you onto others and become a very powerful testimony. I am not one to push my beliefs on others, in fact, I don't tell people enough just how much I rely on God. I have found though that on numerous occasions people ask me how I can be so laid back. I have two answers for them, my mom and God. My mom because she has taught me my whole life that there is someone bigger in control, and I have two options: to worry about things, or just thank God for what He is going to do...I don't know about you, but I would much rather celebrate than be all nervous with worry.

I am truly blessed to have a mother who doesn't judge me, but rather turned me over to God from the beginning. If she had not done this, many times in my journey she would have had a hard time dealing with me and my choices. This would have caused a tremendous strain on our relationship. I see this in so many of my friend's relationships with their parents. Their parents don't approve of their choices, lifestyles, occupations, etc. and they put the children on such an extreme guilt trip. These kids don't have the one supporter in their corner that should absolutely be there. Instead of the parents praising God for their children, and praying for their safety and success, they constantly nag their children and tell them how disappointed they are in them. The saddest part about this is that most of these parents call themselves "Christians." So, what do these kids do, they think that the whole God-thing is a scam, and they never want to hurt someone as their parents are hurting them. I am blessed because my mom always prayed for me instead of judging me, and I am confident that this is why, despite our differences, I can call her my best friend.

When I grow up (I am 34 now), the one thing that I hope people see in me is my mother's beautiful heart. I never hear her gossip, and believe me, this is a rare trait. I never hear her speak unkindly about people, even if I want her to because I feel wronged by them. She instead makes me look at myself, and what I have done to wrong them. There is one thing that I can say about my mom, that I can't say about anyone else that I know. Not once, have I ever heard anyone say a negative thing about her. That makes me most proud to call her my mom.

Juliann

TABLE OF CONTENTS

SIR SORROW

I walked with pleasure many days,
Her touch was soft and gay…
But she could not be trusted
She often let me stray.

But then I met Sir Sorrow,
His touch was firm and strong.
He bent my will and broke my spirit,
And set me back where I belong.

Pleasure taught me not a thing
Though her song I learned to sing,
But Sorrow left me wisdom deep
And placed my soul for God to keep.

By Gladys Rainey Huff
October 1962

This poem was written by my Mother when I was in college. It greatly influenced my understanding of how God uses suffering in our lives.

Trust in the Lord with all your heart,
and do not lean on your own understanding.
In all your ways acknowledge Him,
and He will make your paths straight.
— Proverbs 3:5-6 NAS

INTRODUCTION

*Dear friends, don't be surprised at the
fiery trials you are going through, as
if something strange were happening
to you. Instead, be very glad, because
these trials will make you partners with
Christ in his suffering, and afterward
you will have the wonderful joy of
sharing His glory, when it is displayed
to all the world.*
— *I Peter 4:12-13 NLT*

These verses are for you and for me. The first
two words, "Dear friends," are just what I hope
we will be when you finish this book. As I am
writing, I am thinking about you, the reader, and
how much I want to be able to make your trials
and suffering easier for you to understand. No
one can make your actual trial easier. However,

this book is written to prepare you to be ready and able to walk through the difficulty, knowing that Jesus is walking with you, that He cares, and He will see you through, because He means it for good. We all must suffer, and if we can be prepared, we will not be *surprised* when it comes our way. We need to know that we are not alone and that these *strange* things happen to everyone. Now, you are probably thinking, *Maybe everyone has trials, but you don't know what I am going through. Mine is horrible and it should not be happening to a Christian. It is even worse, because a Christian is causing me to suffer like this. God should not let these things happen to me.*

God says to you, "You are right. In the beginning, I made a perfect world, but my children chose to bring sin into the world and therefore, your life will have suffering. However, I love you so much! I want to work everything out for good for you…if you will let me. I love you so much; I paid the price for you to be my child…a child of the King." God wants to bring good out of your suffering. He wants to give you beauty for ashes.

It means so much to me to know that before I had suffered at all God loved me enough to write the above message to let me know that I **would** have to suffer. When a trial comes our way, the first thing we are tempted to think is, *Poor me, why does this have to happen to me? I'm the only one going through this. Nobody understands. It's not fair to me, me, me, me.* It's pretty normal to think this way. But, there is a bigger picture out there, and if we can grab it, we have a bigger, better way to look at things. That's what this book is about. We will be dear friends by the end, if we can let God pull us up to His perspective, teach us what we need to learn, and help us through our difficulties.

There will be dark storms in all of our lives, and every person's storms are different. Thankfully, our loving God is watching over us and He only allows the storms that will make us better, if we let Him. He wants us to see the sunshine of His love, even in our darkest storm.

You [God], *will keep him in perfect peace, whose mind is stayed on you.*
— *Isaiah 23:3 NKJV*

CHAPTER 1
HOW BIG IS YOUR GOD?

*But thanks be to God! He gives us the
victory through our Lord Jesus Christ.*
— *I Corinthians 15:57 NIV*

*Because of the Lord's great love we
are not consumed, for His compassions
never fail. They are new every morning;
great is Your faithfulness. I say to myself,
"The Lord is my portion; therefore I
will wait for Him." The Lord is good
to those whose hope is in Him to the one
who seeks Him.*

— *Lamentations 3:22-25 NIV*

*Whatever is good and perfect comes to
us from God above, who created all
heaven's lights…He never changes.*

— *James 1:17 NLT*

> *God is not a man, that He should*
> *lie, nor a son of man, that He should*
> *change His mind. Does He speak and*
> *then not act? Does He promise and*
> *not fulfill?*
> — *Numbers 23: 19-20 NIV*

Who is your God? My God loves me more than I can understand, more than the powerful love I feel for my husband, my children, and my grandchildren. He is the blessed controller of all things. He is my helper, best friend, healer, comforter, and father. He is powerful, protective, providing, pure, almighty, amazing, faithful, and wonderful. He understands me, knows all the answers, and loves to give me wisdom. He wants to work everything out for my good and His glory. I could write a whole book on how big God is, and still not cover all of His wonderful attributes.

It is good to remember and meditate on Who God is. When I cannot go to sleep at night, I start with the letter "A" and think of all the words and phrases that describe God beginning with the letter "A." Then I go to "B" and on through the alphabet. Most nights I fall asleep long before I get to "Z."

Psalm 23, 103, and 139 are good Psalms on which to meditate. Memorize scripture that means a lot to you. However you do it, spend time each day meditating on your God and how big He is.

When your time of suffering comes, you will be much better off if you already see God as the wonderful controller of your life. Then you will be able to accept what He lovingly allows in your life.

Several months ago, our daughter-in-law's father was told that he had lung cancer. He told me that if this had happened to him 9 years ago, before he became a Christian, he would have been very angry, and he would have made everyone around him miserable. He said,

> "My feelings then would have been, it's my life, and this can't be happening to me. The big difference, now that I'm a Christian, is in **accepting** what happens to me. I don't own me anymore. If you truly give your life to God and let Him direct it, you may not necessarily like or agree with what is happening to you, but you accept it (as from God). We don't have to understand why.

The problem for me is people who claim to be Christians, but they portray a poor image of what Christians are supposed to be. You can't tell God, **I'll give you my life IF…, or on these conditions.** This causes you to wrestle with God. I have peace about what is happening to me; I know that it is a "win-win" situation. If I am healed, or if I go on to Heaven, I'll be a winner."

We are praying for his healing, and we have been blessed as we have watched him trust in God to handle his health and show His love to everyone he can. Instead of giving in to his pain and suffering, he is constantly out doing something for someone else. He has accepted his illness and is doing all he can to glorify God in his suffering.

CHAPTER 2
ONE MISERABLE YEAR

One year and 2 months after our first date we became engaged!! I was 23 years old and so excited. My life had been pretty perfect until then, and it was only going to get better. I loved God. I was happy. Life was great! I had fallen in love with the most brilliant, fun, good-looking, and wonderful man in the whole world…and he had fallen in love with me. He was a preacher, and we both loved the Lord and wanted to serve Him; life could only get better. I started planning, and April 8 seemed to be the perfect wedding day, until I mentioned it to Eddie. He was not sure. Two months later, he still was not sure. And two months later, he just could not set a date. He told me that he had to know what God wanted, and he did not have an answer. I was getting a little frustrated. God had already told ME, and couldn't Eddie just take MY word for it?! Well, NO, he could not!!

Eddie was my wonderful Prince Charming, but for the first time in my life, after 6 months of trying to talk him into setting a wedding date, he was making my life miserable. I was suffering. Do you know how it feels to want something really bad, and not get it? I was even sure it was God's will, and the man I loved was telling me to wait; I just did not get it. I became more and more miserable.

You have probably suffered in some way in your life, too. You may be suffering now. There is so much sickness, loneliness, neglect, financial pressure, job insecurity, and pain of every kind. Marital problems, divorce, children problems, disasters, and accidents are in every family. Life holds suffering for everyone. Some feel the pains early, some later, but all will feel the pain. Some suffering comes as a result of our own actions, but much comes as a result of life in this world. This book is about suffering. Why does God, who loves us more than we can imagine, allow all of this suffering?

We tend to focus on ourselves and our problems, but there is a much bigger picture. God wants to help us see the big picture, but we are usually more concerned with <u>our</u> picture, <u>our</u> lives, <u>our</u> plans, <u>our</u> desires, <u>our</u> wants, the people we love…but I am learning that it is not about us. That is not an easy lesson to learn, but with God's help, it can be learned, and the big picture becomes more clear. It is <u>not</u> about me; it <u>is</u> about God.

He is in control of the big picture, and if we are His children, He is working in our lives for good. He wants to take away our independence, pride, and ungodliness, and make us into His image. He wants to use our trials to help us develop the fruit of the Spirit: love, joy, peace, patience, kindness, goodness, faithfulness, gentleness, and self-control in our lives. He waits for us to cooperate with Him, by trusting Him to know and do the right thing. He wants us to give Him our plans, our desires, our pain, OUR LIFE!

Romans 12:12 says we should, *"Be glad for all God is planning for you. Be patient in trouble, and always be prayerful."* If we can relax in His love and wait on His plan, we will know the joy and fulfillment He gives to those whose hope is in Him.

In July, we got our marriage license; I thought I had almost won. Then Eddie said he still did not feel God's permission to go ahead with the wedding. After one whole year of my frustration, coercing, fussing, manipulating, depression, tears, fears, and complaints, I was totally at the end of myself. Now, that is a good place to be, because that is when we turn to God. Or do we? Sometimes we do, and sometimes we do not. If we have learned that God loves us and has a perfect plan for our lives, and if we have given our lives completely to Him, then we know that the best thing we can do is trust Him to work it out. It may mean that I will not get what I wanted, but I will get God's best. I had prayed a lot during that year, because I really did love God and want His will, but I wanted Him to want my plan. God gives the best to those who leave the choice to Him.

A few days before Christmas when I was lower than I had ever been in my 24 years, I bowed my head and said,

> *"God, this is too hard for me. I thought I was fighting for Your will. I was so sure You wanted this marriage, but it is making me sick, and I am totally worn out. I give my life completely to You. I surrender all, even if it means not spending the rest of my life with the man I love. I am sick of trying*

*to get my way, I'm sick of me, and I give
You permission to do whatever You want in
my life."*

As I prayed and cried and listened, I felt God asking me to let Eddie go. I felt that God was telling me that He had to be the most important thing in my life, and I could show Him this by letting go of what I wanted. Did I trust God that much? Could He give me a life that was better than the one I was struggling so hard to get?

Our faith and trust in God is based on one of two facts: 1. Who God is, OR, 2. What God does. When we focus on the blessings we want God to give us, we are basing our faith on what God does. Since God sees the big picture, we cannot base our faith on what we see God doing.

I knew who my God was, and I knew I served a BIG God. My mother, my Sunday School, and Training Union teachers in the church where I grew up had lovingly taught me about Who God is: His love, power, might, and mercy. And I knew I should keep my focus on Who God is.

GIVE MY DESIRES TO GOD

Years earlier I had memorized Psalm 37:4, *"Delight yourself in the Lord, and He will give you the desires of your heart."* During that year, I was focused on what God was doing or, more accurately, what God was NOT doing. I kept telling myself that if I would delight myself in the Lord, He would give me the desires of my heart. Do we think God wants to give us whatever our hearts desire?

Do you think parents should give their children whatever their hearts desire? NO! NO! We have a good God, and He is big enough to NOT give us everything our hearts desire. Sometimes, when I am in the middle of a trial, I am like a spoiled child and I don't like it when God tells me, "No," or "Wait." But when I am not in a trial, I see more clearly, and I love God, because He does not always let me have what I want. I love Him for being the Blessed Controller of all things, for being aware of all the things I cannot see, and for taking care of me. I want to get to the place where I give God every trial at the beginning, and ask Him to use it to teach me what He wants me to learn.

God was trying to teach me that if I would really delight myself in Him (in who He is, not what He does), I would be so delighted with Him that I could let my desires go, and then He could fill my heart with His desires. It is like when parents plan a wonderful surprise for a child, and the child desires to sit and watch his "favorite TV program." The child doesn't know that something much, much better than the TV is waiting for him. If the parents do not tell him they have the surprise, and they only tell him to cut off the TV and come now...there will probably be the same fuss, argument, bad attitude, exasperated expressions, questioning, etc., that we display toward God when we want to do our own thing. But, we too miss the surprise. That is what I had done for a whole year. I acted like a spoiled child who wanted God to give me what I wanted, the way I wanted it. It was only when I gave my desires to God, and asked Him to do His will in my life, that I felt peace and joy again.

DO NOT WORRY ABOUT ANYTHING

The other scripture I held onto was:

> *Don't worry about anything, but in*
> *everything by prayer and supplication,*
> *with thanksgiving; let your requests be*
> *made known to God. And the peace*
> *that passes all understanding will*
> *guard your heart and mind in*
> *Christ Jesus.*
> — *Philippians 4:6-7 NAS*

I had spent a whole year *worrying* my prayers, *worrying* that our marriage was not happening according to plan (whose plan?), *worrying, worrying, worrying...* God was trying to teach me that I could tell Him what I wanted, then I could relax and concentrate on being thankful for who God is, and for the fact that He loved Eddie and me, and that He would handle it for us.

My worries had caused me to focus on myself and what I wanted/needed. It made me neglect everything and everybody God had given me to bless. When we get so selfish that all we can think about is our hurt and our needs, our hearts grow hard, our faces get drawn, hard, and unattractive, and we do not even realize it. I have been there.

When the smile does not come easily, I know that I am focused on me and not on God. What about you when you cannot smile? **When you are in pain, ask yourself where your focus is.** Are you looking to God to see what amazing things He is doing in your life, or are you looking at your problem, and drowning in it? I am just asking you to **focus on who God is, not on your hurt.** When I lose myself in God and His goodness, His word, and praising Him, when I can stop worrying, planning, fretting, controlling and just let God be God, I can go beyond my hurts to the world and its hurts, and my family and friends and their hurts. I can have the confidence that God is going to take care of what concerns me, and I can be free to unselfishly let Him use me to help others. That is when the peace and joy come back. That is when I can smile, even though it hurts. You can, too. I am not saying that there will never be tears, because there will. But after you dry your eyes, if you look to Jesus, He will be there for you.

When I looked to Jesus, I knew what I had to do. I had to give Eddie and my future to God; I had to trust Him with my life.

On Christmas Day afternoon, I gave the engagement ring back to Eddie and told him I felt God told me to give up, to stop what I had tried so hard to get, and to let him go. I assured him that I loved him and wanted to spend the rest of my life with him. But I felt God was telling me that I could not see him again, unless he knew God was ready for us to get married. When he took me home, I was so sad to think I might never see him again, but so relieved to know that I could relax and trust God to handle my life. I felt like a million pounds had been lifted off my shoulders, and I was happy to be rid of the pressure to make life happen the way I thought it should. I am sure Eddie was relieved, too, because I had been worse than a dripping faucet for the past year. My face had become drawn and ugly. I was always too tired to be any fun, because I had been so selfishly concerned about getting what I wanted. That was 40 years ago, and do you think I have been totally faithful in letting God handle my life since then? I wish I could say, "Yes," but even though He is much better at being in charge than I, I have messed up by trying to be in charge of my life numerous times. I can make myself so miserable over the smallest of things, and I'll bet you can, too. When I try to be in charge, I cause a lot of my own suffering.

Well, back to our story. The day after Christmas, I left town to go visit friends, because I could not bear to be in the same town as Eddie and not be together. On New Year's Day I went home. When I walked in the door, Mother told me Eddie had called, and I needed to return his call. I didn't know what to do; it had been clear to both of us that we would not even talk unless God told him we could get married. I called; he came over.

He said, "I'm ready to get married."

I asked, "When?"

He casually replied, "Any time you want to."

I thought I was dreaming, but answered, "Tomorrow. **No! Tonight!**"

Eddie called the pastor-friend we had asked long ago to marry us, and they arranged for us to get married as soon as we could get there. (Remember, we had gotten our marriage license in July!) We got both of our families together, drove 30 miles to the church, and were married at 11:00 that night!!! The pastor's wife played the organ, and they had a florist decorate the church (even down to the aisle runner). They even had a professional photographer. When you leave it up to God, He is amazing! We had everything most couples spend six months planning for. And the price was right!! Yes, we are grateful to the pastor and his wife; they are still close friends. My smile was suddenly brighter than ever!! I am still so amazed at what God will do when I get out of the way.

Do we have a calm, uneventful, boring life? No! It's been pretty exciting for 40 years. Have we suffered? Yes, lots! But we learn a little more each time we give our problems to God.

CHAPTER 3
FAMILY SUFFERING

By the next New Year's Day, on our first anniversary, we were so in love, and we were going to have a baby! It would be the first grandchild on both sides!!! Eddie was almost 31 and I was 25; we were old enough to be more than a little excited. Both our families were praising God and thanking Him for His goodness to all of us.

One Sunday night in April, about a week before the baby was due, Eddie was preaching a revival in another town, and I went to our church alone. The baby hadn't moved for several days, and I thought he must be resting and getting ready to come. I was concerned that my water might break at church or that the baby would come while I was sleeping, and I would wake up having a baby and not know what to do. The pastor preached the message using one of the Psalms. I have no idea which one he read, but I was gradually filled with the realization that something had happened to our baby. God filled me with peace and assurance that He was in control, and that I could trust Him. I didn't tell Eddie anything when he called that night. He would leave for home in the morning, and we would be together in the afternoon; by then I would know for sure. I had a doctor's appointment Monday morning, and even though I wanted to be brave, I called my mother to go with me. When the doctor could not get a heart beat and sent me for tests, I was numb. Mother suffered with me when they told us the baby was not living. It had been a perfectly healthy baby, but very active, and the umbilical cord had knotted, and the baby had died. We went home to wait for Eddie. I would tell him the news, and we would get through this dark time together.

Eddie came in with big smiles and a load of baby presents. The church had given us a Baby Shower and so many baby gifts. One of the hardest things I have ever had to do was tell him that our baby was not living. Tears come even now as I think about it. We cried, and we prayed, and we cried some more. But, thankfully, we had grown to the point that our faith was based on who God is, and not on what He is doing. We got on our knees and thanked God that He was with us, and that He knew what He was doing. He had chosen us to go through this tragedy instead of someone who did not know Him and might get mad at Him. We knew He was in control, and we were able to look at the big picture and claim Romans 8:28. I must have reminded myself that, "All things work together for good to those that love God"…all things, ALL things, ALL THINGS, hundreds of times during those days. We continually reminded each other that God knew what He was doing.

My doctor tried to induce labor, but it did not work. He told us we would just have to go home, and wait for me to go into labor naturally. Waiting was very dangerous, because the baby was decaying, and that put my life in danger. I carried the baby 3 more weeks, and the hardest part was when people asked me when my baby was due. At first, I tried to explain, but that brought tears every time. I learned to try to smile, and say, "Last week."

Eddie was so kind and loving to me during those days, but there was the temptation for me to selfishly suffer. I told myself that I had every right to a "pity party" when I felt like I needed it, *"because it wasn't fair; we would have been good loving parents, we were getting so old, we really wanted a baby, and all the other thoughts that came into our heads when we were thinking about self."* There were good days, and then there were dark days. Thankfully, I knew who God was, and the devil's temptations to wallow in my sadness were resisted most of the time. Gradually, peace and trust in God's faithfulness made us able to smile again.

God's plan to take our child has been so valuable to us when we have been with parents who have lost a child. We know the feelings, and we also know the God who gives and the God who takes away. We don't know why He does what He does, but we know who God is and that He does not make mistakes. We also know that our suffering is part of His plan.

We can tell other parents that it is OK to be sad, and that they will miss their child. I still think about him on his birthday, and other times, too. I try to imagine what he would be like and what he would be doing now. But I am not angry at God; He knows so much more than I know, and He knows why it was best for Him to take our baby. I am thankful He is in control.

Soon we were excited about another baby (or babies?)! The day we found out I was pregnant again, we saw two of the most perfect rainbows we had ever seen. They were in the sky together, and I was so excited. I knew that God was telling me we were going to have twins, to make up for the one we lost. Yes, I'm a dreamer! With God all things are possible, but we did not have twins. We had a perfect baby boy, a gift from God. Then, two years later we had a perfect baby girl, another gift from God. He is so good; we were so blessed.

Twelve years ago, God blessed us with a perfect daughter-in-law. Our children are a special blessing to us.

You may be wondering about our "perfect" children. God gave them to us, and that makes them perfect for us. They are not really perfect; only God is perfect.

I have a friend who has lost three babies and is concerned that she may never be able to have children. I am so sad for her. She would be a wonderful mother, and it does not make sense that she would not have children. I have to remember that God sees the big picture, and He does not make mistakes. His plan may be to bless her in a different way, or He may be teaching her some important lessons now and bless her with children later. He may need her to mother children that she did not birth. We do not know His plan, but we do know His plan is for good. God gives the best to those who leave the choice to Him. Ask God to help you leave the choices in your life to Him.

CHAPTER 4
EVERYDAY SUFFERING

Eddie had been an evangelist, traveling from church to church, during the first five years of our marriage; then he felt like God was calling him to start a church. So we moved to Augusta, Georgia, and we started a church. He is a great preacher, and we were privileged to be a part of a church where God really showed His power, glory, and majesty. Soon he was pastoring a very big church, full of wonderful people. God was using us, and life was good. The devil does not like that, and he does all he can to cause our testimony to crumble.

We enjoyed what God was doing in our midst, but we also experienced a lot of suffering. I am sure that you have experienced suffering in your life, too. I want you to think about your suffering, your problems, and your trials. The actual trials and suffering we all experience are not what is important. What is important is how we learn to respond to the suffering.

> *Consider it all joy, my brethren, when you encounter various trials, knowing that the testing of your faith produces endurance. And let endurance have its perfect result, that you may be perfect and complete, lacking in nothing. But if anyone lacks wisdom, let him ask of God, who gives to all men generously and without reproach, and it will be given to him. But let him ask in faith, without doubting, for the one who doubts is like the surf of the sea driven and tossed by the wind. For let not that man expect that he will receive anything from the Lord being a double-minded man, unstable in all his ways.*
> — *James 1:2-8 NAS*

This was the first scripture I memorized during this time of suffering. Please read it in every version you have, because that will help you understand it better. Try to understand it before you have your next trial, so that you will be able to welcome the trial as a gift.

"How do I consider it 'pure joy' when I am facing these trials?" I would ask God over and over. Then I would go to verse 5 and tell God that He promised wisdom to anyone who would ask Him <u>without doubting</u>. I had no doubts that He had the answers, but I had to believe that He wanted to give them to me. As I began to hear direction from God, my faith increased. The more I depended on Him for the answers, the more He gave them to me, usually through His Word.

He loves for us to look away from our problem and look to Him in the Bible. My Bibles (I love to read different versions and paraphrases) became my best friends. God will give you wisdom, too. But you must remember who God is, and know that He has the answers and that He wants to tell them to you. I had to learn that the best way for me to learn who God is was to read the letter He had written to me, and the best way for me to find His answers were in that same letter. He wrote the Bible to us as a letter to tell us all we need to know to live as a Princess, a child of the King.

If you are not reading your Bible daily, pray and ask God to help you find the time to read it. Ask Him to give you a desire for His Word.

Humility is not thinking less of yourself
It is thinking of yourself less.

CHAPTER 5
A GENTLE AND QUIET SPIRIT

You know how a little child takes a broken toy to his mom and confidently waits for her to fix it? He knows she will have it for a little while and then he will get it back fixed and ready to be played with again. There are some children who give it to Mom to be fixed, but they try to tell her how to do it; they pull on her hands, and pull on the toy, and try to fix it themselves. Mom cannot do a thing until the child finally gives up and gives her the toy. We are like that with God. We have to quietly and patiently give our hurts to God and wait for Him to fix us.

Once we had a big problem. The pain was bad and the time was dark, but God wanted me to give it to Him, so He could do what was best. I was selfishly focused on me and how it was affecting me, and again I was becoming hard and ugly. I held on to my hurts and became too self-centered to notice anyone else's hurts. But I thought I was hiding my hurt and frustration, even from Eddie. I thought I was dealing with the problem with God alone. I was praying fervently, but again I was telling Him how to settle the issue. As always, the frustration of trying to make life happen according to "my plan" left me tired, grouchy, and hurting. I was just like the child who tries to fix it himself. I would not give up and look up. Then we went to a conference in Atlanta, and that night as we were walking to the car I heard Eddie lovingly say, "You need exactly what the speaker talked about tonight."

"What?" I asked.

"You know, a gentle and quiet spirit," he calmly offered.

I became livid! How could he dare to tell me (who was screaming silently in hurt and desperation), that I needed God's quiet and gentle spirit?

I went home and looked the words up in my dictionary. Gentle means having a mild or kind nature, to cause someone to become less agitated by means of words or actions.

Quiet means to be free from trouble or disturbance, displaying calmness and self control, relaxing and peaceful. I was just the opposite!! Well, he was right, as usual.

It was not easy for me to accept my need, but over the next weeks, as I ate and drank I Peter 3, God blessed me (and Eddie and our children, I am sure) by teaching me how to have a gentle and quiet spirit. I learned to hand the problem to God, and wait patiently and quietly as He fixed it and me.

> *In the same way, you wives must accept the authority of your husbands, even those who refuse to accept the good news. Your Godly lives will speak to them better than any words. They will by won over by watching your pure Godly behavior. Don't be concerned about the outward beauty that depends on fancy hairstyles, expensive jewelry, or beautiful clothes. You should be known for the beauty that comes from within, the unfading beauty of a gentle and quiet spirit, which is so precious to God.*
> — *I Peter 3:1-6 NLT*

A gentle and quiet spirit is precious to God, (some versions say a gentle and quiet spirit is beautiful to God), and I wanted my spirit to be precious and beautiful to God. According to I Peter 3, I had to learn to:

1. Be submissive to my husband and accept His authority. God did not say this because I was inferior to my husband, but because it is necessary in the order of the home. God holds the husband responsible for being the Head of the Home and for making the final decisions for the good of the family. I think He wants the wife to be the Heart of the Home, and that requires a gentle and quiet spirit.

2. Live a Godly life, and do what is right. A Godly life speaks more loudly than words. Actions speak louder than words.

3. Be more concerned with inner beauty than outward beauty.

4. Trust God so much that there is no fear in my life. God's perfect love frees us of fear; we must know Him enough to give Him our fears, and trust in His love and His care. When we have no fear, we naturally have a more gentle and quiet spirit.

It took prayer, and more prayer, but God had allowed a trial that gave me an opportunity to practice all of the above things, and He was with me to help me learn. I could have fought the trial, but I am so glad I gave it to God, and let Him give me a gentle and quiet spirit in the process.

The whole book of I Peter has become so special to me, because it has taught me that suffering is not something we need to fight or to fear.

> *In this you greatly rejoice, though now for a little while you may have had to suffer grief in all kinds of trials. These have come so that your faith — of greater worth than gold, which perishes even though refined by fire — may be proved genuine and may result in praise, glory, and honor when Jesus Christ is revealed.*
> — *I Peter 1:6-7 NIV*

We do suffer grief in all kinds of trials on this earth, but we can greatly rejoice that it's only for a little while in the big picture of eternity. And we rejoice that our faith is proven genuine through our trials. We are refined by our fires.

Can we say, "Bring on the trials? I give up my right to have life like I want it, Lord. I'll accept the suffering that comes my way, and let You use it to refine me and make me the best person I can possibly be."

I do not want this book to cause you guilt and condemnation. I do not want it to make you hurt more. I want you to realize that there is a better way, and it is the way God planned for you. He wants to love you, protect you, and take care of you, but He wants you to love Him with all your heart and soul and mind so you will want to obey Him.

CHAPTER 6
HAPPINESS COMES FROM WHERE?

Early in our marriage, I would be so happy when Eddie would do things for me, listen to me, be there for me, etc., but soon my expectations grew to expect him to make me happy. I didn't even realize this was happening, but suddenly, if he was not there to do what I wanted, when I wanted it, I was unhappy...and I blamed him. Now, this is an example of Eddie suffering for doing right, because he was not intentionally hurting me. He was just going to work, providing for his family, loving us, and taking care of everything he had to take care of without realizing that I had come to expect the impossible from him. There was no way he could have won this battle, because no person can make another person truly happy. People can make us feel good for awhile, but not forever. I am embarrassed to say that I did all the things we do when we think someone else is responsible for our unhappiness. I tried to reason with him, pouted, fretted, whined, grew quiet, and whatever else we do, and of course, it just grew worse. I was making Eddie suffer, and we were both getting miserable. I finally begged God for an answer, and He is good. As I was reading Psalms (the book I read most when I am suffering), He gradually showed me that my joy and my happiness must come from Him. As soon as I grasped that wisdom, I asked God to forgive me for trying to find happiness apart from Him, and I asked Eddie to forgive me for expecting him to give me something that was impossible for him to give me. I asked God to help me notice all the things that Eddie did for me, and to help me show him my gratitude. This life is really hard sometimes, and we need to be there for each other, loving and encouraging each other. We need to be grateful to the people in our lives and to God.

This has been one of the most important lessons I have ever learned, and one I pray you will always remember. **No person can make you happy.** Real happiness comes from your relationship with God. People depend on money, things, trips, relationships and so forth to make them happy. It just can't happen, because God planned from the beginning to be the source of our happiness.

> *You have made known to me the path of life, you will fill me with joy in your presence, with eternal pleasures at your right hand.*
> — *Psalm 16:11 NIV*

CHAPTER 7
LORD, CHANGE ME

God is so good, because He does not give us a list of all the things that are wrong in our lives when we are saved. We would feel so defeated if He told us all that needed changing at once. He shows us how to change one thing at a time to make us more like Christ. Soon after I learned that my happiness must come from God, I read a book by Evelyn Christenson, *Lord Change Me*.

There were a lot of tears and prayers when I realized that whenever someone did something that bothered me, it was probably God using them to help me change. When someone did something that bothered me and I was ready to ask God to change THEM, she said I was supposed to ask God to change ME!!! I know, I rebelled at first, too. But, now I know she is right. We need to focus on God and what He wants to do, instead of on us and what we want. The big picture, remember?

But the little picture is important here, too. I am a little part of the picture that God is painting for His glory. I must yield to Him, and let Him paint me in His way, not my way. Every time I don't like something that another person does, I try to remember to ask God if that has come to my attention to change me. I have prayed many prayers for God to change another person, only to end with the surrender of my will, and the words, "Lord, change me, and make me what you want me to be."

CHAPTER 8
MY PORTION

As God was changing me and stripping me of some of the selfish and ugly that was part of me, I learned another important lesson. We all have the feeling sometimes that things are not fair.

> *"It's not fair for my boss to give me all this extra work. It's not fair for me to have to work extra hours. It's not fair for me to have to pick up my husband's clothes. It's not fair for me to do all I have to do for my children. It's not fair for my friend to get to have more than me. It's not fair for me to have to do something for a neighbor who has never done anything for me.*

We think we deserve more or better, or at least something else. One of the first things I taught my children was that, **Life is Not Fair!!**

God struck me with a scripture that I now love; I say struck, because when I read it I felt like I had been struck with lightning. It was so bright and clear to me. Psalm 73:26 and Psalm 119:57 both tell me that God is my portion. That may not be a big deal to you, but I grew up in a family with five children. I was always concerned about being fair and everybody having the right portion. I am sure I was really concerned with my getting as much as the others did when it came to cookies or pie, and I was concerned about not getting more than everyone else when it came to the work we were required to do. (That's a story for another book, because I grew up on a farm, and there was always a lot of work to do.) It shows my selfishness, but I must tell you that I had always been concerned about MY portion. Suddenly, I understood that God was my portion. WOW! There was nothing better and nothing more that I could ask for. God was my portion, all and more than I could ever ask for.

Think about it! If God is your portion, you do not need anything more. God is my portion, and all the other things I thought I needed or wanted are not really necessary. I have all that is necessary to make me happy, satisfied, content, and pleased. "God is my portion, all and more than I deserve," became my motto. Now, can you see how much better that makes my life, if I already have more than I deserve? Jesus suffered death on a cruel cross so that I could have eternal life. That is **more than I deserve!!** Everything else is a blessing. Everything my husband does for me is wonderful and extra. Eddie does not have to make me happy, because God is my portion, and Eddie and his love are above and beyond. My children do not have to make me happy, because God is my portion, and my children are extra joys that God has allowed and blessed me with. My friends do not have to make me happy…And when someone does something that I don't like or that makes me suffer, God reminds me that He is my portion; they are not supposed to live their life for me. I need to look to Him, and I don't need to worry about making someone else meet my needs. God loves me and is taking care of me. He loves them and is taking care of them, also.

Ask God to help you understand how good it is when He is your portion. Ask Him to help you be satisfied with Him. Of course, I am not perfect, and I forget. When I get focused on myself and miserable, I realize that I must have slipped away from my first love. God reminds me that He is my portion.

There is no better portion; He's the best, and you can have Him, too. God is your portion, all and more than you deserve. When you can accept Him as your portion, you do not **expect** anything else from your husband, children, co-workers, or anyone to make your life better. You will be able to see the things people do for you as extras, and you will begin to appreciate the people in your life much more. Jesus is the cake, and everything else is like icing on the cake.

Think about Jesus being your portion, (all and more than you deserve), and think about all of the unfulfilled expectations you have and are holding on to. Can you give them to God and tell Him that you accept Him as your portion? Can you tell Him you will be grateful if He gives you the things you think you want? Can you tell Him that if He does not give them to you, you will still be grateful to Him, because you know He knows what is best for you? This will make your life so much better. You will begin to see your husband, children, and everyone else as wonderful additions to your life (the icing on your cake).

We all have desires that make us hurt and suffer when they are not met. Yours may be a new house, a husband, a baby, a new job, a ministry, furniture, health, or whatever. These desires are different for each of us. Try to take your eyes off 'the prize' (the thing you are longing for), and focus on your real Prize: Jesus is your portion, all and more than you deserve.

Ask Him to help you begin to see the blessings you already have and to make you grateful for each of them. Read Lamentations 3:22-25 in your Bible or in the scripture at the beginning of chapter 1.

The Lord is my portion;
Therefore I will wait for Him.

— *Lamentations 3:24 NIV*

CHAPTER 9
SUFFERING FOR DOING GOOD

*For it is commendable if a man bears
up under the pain of unjust suffering
because he is conscious of God. But
how is it to your credit if you receive
a beating for doing wrong and endure
it? But if you suffer for doing good and
you endure it, this is commendable
before God. To this you were called,
because Christ suffered for you, leaving
you an example that you should follow
in His steps.*

— *I Peter 2:19-21 NIV*

SUFFERING FOR DOING WRONG

One day, when I felt like my suffering was so unfair, I read I Peter 2:19. It is <u>rewritten</u> below with <u>my comments</u>:

> *For it is commendable if a man or woman bears up under the pain of unjust suffering because he or she is conscious of God. But how is it to your credit if you receive a beating for doing wrong and endure it?* (I had certainly not been beaten, and hopefully, neither have you. This was written for slaves who were beaten at this time in history, but I could easily substitute the words "if you are hurting" for "if you receive a beating".) *But if you suffer for doing good and you endure it, this is commendable before God.*

As I contemplated this scripture, I realized that I had done wrong and that I needed to stop enduring it. **I needed to stop doing wrong!!**

You may be guilty of doing wrong, too. We are not perfect; we all have our "pet sins." We all do wrong. Pray and ask God to show you anything you are doing, or even thinking, that is wrong. It could be something that everyone else is aware of, but you are not even aware of. Or it could be something that only you (and God) know. But God will allow it to cause you pain, to get your attention. You **can** give your sin(s) to God and stop enduring the pain, because **you <u>can</u> stop doing whatever you are doing that is wrong.** It may be hard to stop doing something you are doing wrong; it may have even become a bad habit. The Bible says in Philippians 4:13, *"I can do all things through Christ who strengthens me."*

SUFFERING FOR DOING GOOD

This is so neat to me: *"If you suffer for doing good and you endure it, this is commendable before God."* I can make God happy; I can cause Him joy! I can give God pleasure. I can do something that makes Him proud of me! What exactly is it? Read on... *"To this you were called, because Christ suffered for you, leaving you an example that you should follow in His steps."* I Peter 2:21

If I patiently endure unfair treatment because I want to obey God, He is pleased. Christ suffered for me and asked me to suffer for Him, but **He gave me an example of how to do it His way.**

> *He committed no sin, and no deceit*
> *was found in His mouth. When they*
> *hurled their insults at Him, He did*
> *not retaliate; when He suffered He*
> *made no threats. Instead He entrusted*
> *Himself to Him who judges justly.*
> — *I Peter 3:22-23*

- He did good
- He did not sin
- He did not deceive anyone
- He did not retaliate when He was insulted
- He did not threaten to get even
- He left His case in the hands of God who always judges fairly.

Now read what Jesus said in Luke:

> *Love your enemies. Do good to those*
> *who hate you. Pray for the happiness*
> *of those who hurt you. If someone*
> *slaps you on one cheek, turn the other*
> *cheek. If someone demands your coat,*
> *offer your shirt also. Give what you*

have to anyone who asks you for it;
and when things are taken away from
you, don't try to get them back. Do
for others as you would like them to do
for you.
— *Luke 6:27-31 NLT*

According to what we read in Luke 6, Jesus also asks us to:

- Love our enemies
- Do good to those who hate you
- Pray for the happiness of those who hurt you
- Pray for those who hurt you
- Turn the other cheek
- Give what you have
- When something is taken from you, don't try to get it back
- Do unto others as you want them to do to you

As you are starting to think, *"But Lord, you don't know my situation, this is just too hard for me,"* He tells us more:

> *Do you think you deserve credit merely for loving those who love you? Even sinners do that! And if you do good only to those who do good to you, is that so wonderful? Even sinners do that much!...God is kind to the unthankful and to those who are wicked. You must be compassionate just as your Father is compassionate.*
> — Luke 6:32-33, 36 NLT

God is kind to those who do not even know Him or thank Him. He is kind to those who do know Him, but do not thank Him. Can I do that? Can I be kind to my husband when he does not thank me for all the things I do for him? Can I be kind to others who do not appreciate me?

Surely you do not want me to act like you, Jesus, or do you? I can hear Him softly saying, *"If you love me, you will act like me, I will be with you, and great will be your reward in Heaven."* It will be hard to do good to someone who has done you wrong, or to love someone who does not love you, or pray for someone who is hurting you. These things are so against our nature that we really do suffer as we are trying to do the right thing. Doing it God's way is so hard that you cannot do it alone; you must have His help.

HOW DO I GET HIS HELP?

When you love, pray for, give to, or do good to someone who is hurting you, you will have to **ASK** for God's power and strength. He is so good to give what we need: He can fill us with love when we have none. He wants us to be the channel He can use to pour out His love, strength, mercy, kindness, and power on others. Does this seem impossible to you? It is impossible to love others (especially those who hurt us) in our own strength and power. We can only do it with Jesus, in us, helping us to act like Him. And the neatest thing of all is that He rewards us for doing it His way. The reward may be the personal satisfaction of knowing the anger you would normally feel is no longer there, or it could be added to your rewards in Heaven. It could be peace and joy, or whatever God wants to give you. He is so good.

There have been many times when I have prayed for God to bless people who hurt me (because God asked me to). God tells us to love, even our enemies. We sometimes think that we do not have any enemies, but actually our enemies are anyone we are having a hard time loving. Sometimes I get so upset with my "enemies," that I have to pray for God to love them through me. When I don't feel like I can show them any love at the time, I have to ask God to love my husband, children, family, and friends through me. Do you sometimes have a hard time loving your family and friends? You will be amazed at how well God can love them through you, <u>if you ask Him, and then cooperate with Him.</u>

It is amazing that God can actually **give** you love for someone. I have seen it happen many times. Pray and ask God to fill you with love for whoever is hard (even impossible) for you to love. **Expect Him** to give you the love, and **thank Him** for giving you the love. **Continually pray for God to bless the person.** Focus on the good things you can think of in that person. God **will** fill you with love if you let Him. God is love.

CHAPTER 10
APPLICATION AND EXAMPLES

Think of some of the ways we suffer when we are not doing wrong, and remind yourself how God wants you to handle it. What are the right ways to respond?

SCENARIO #1

You are doing your best in your job, but your boss is making it difficult for you. Will you act like Jesus and, with all the help God gives you, commit no sin, make no threats, do no wrong, and leave it in God's hands? This will be hard! It will be so hard that you will feel pain and suffering, but this is the suffering God has called us to; it is suffering for Him. I have seen God do mighty miracles in many lives when the one who is treated unfairly responds God's way. How will you respond?

SCENERIO # 2

Someone you work with is jealous of you, or unfair, or mean to you. This happens all of the time, and it causes all kinds of suffering for you. But you must do no wrong, do not try to get even, retaliate, or threaten; you must endure lovingly.

Look at Luke 6. What should you do?

1.

2.

3.

4.

SCENERIO #3

Your parents/children make you suffer by being so demanding. (I know at least 10 people personally whose parents are making them suffer terribly. Some are so old that they may not even know what they are doing, but never the less my friends are suffering.) Your suffering is commendable to God if you do no wrong (because you are a child of God).

You pray and seek strength from Him,

- Do not deceive.
- Do not retaliate.
- Do not threaten.
- Do your best to show the love of Christ.
- Let God handle the situation.

I am not saying you should let them do exactly as they please and continue to hurt you. But you must lovingly allow God to give you the wisdom to know how to love them. You cannot make them happy, or healthy, or fix them in any way. But you can show the love of God to them, and to all who are watching, as you respond to suffering the way Jesus did. Speaking the truth in love, you will possibly have to use tough love and say, "No," to them sometimes.

What will you do in your situation?

1.

2.

3.

4.

SCENERIO #4

Your husband/wife won't communicate with you, does everything he/she can to make your life miserable, embarrasses you, deserts the family, or has an affair. You will suffer if any of the above happens to you, but you do not have to grow bitter, jealous, selfish, or vengeful.

Remember, you must do no wrong:

- Do not sin.
- Do not deceive.
- Do not retaliate when insulted.
- Do not threaten to get even.

What can you do? Leave it in the hands of God who always judges fairly, and seek His wisdom. Every person's case is different. That is why God asks us to seek Him and His wisdom and understanding. He wants to bless us with His help and presence, but not uninvited. He likes to have our invitation to show us His power. How would you handle this problem?

CHAPTER 11
THE WORST SUFFERING

The worst suffering of all comes when something bad has happened to you, and you cannot forgive the person (or persons) who you think caused it, and then, as an act of your will, let it go. If you have not forgiven, you cannot let it go, and go on with the rest of your life. I have a friend who is the most beautiful example of forgiveness and letting go that I have ever seen. When I asked her to explain how she was able to do this, she wrote:

> First, let me make sure you realize my ability to forgive only comes by the grace of God. I am just as human as you are, and I know I have let God down so many times with my responses to different unpleasant situations in my life. However, I am

trying to grow to be more like Him in the area of forgiveness.

You know, God doesn't necessarily want bad things to happen to us, but He gave us all a free will, and many times that free will demonstrates a lot of selfishness that will cause "bad things" to happen in our lives. God is so good to us that He often tries to prepare us for unpleasant situations that <u>He</u> sees coming, before we ever know anything about them. The situation I'm about to share with you is where God really began to test my faith, draw me closer to Him, and teach me what it really meant to be a "living witness" for Him, while demonstrating more forgiveness than was humanly possible.

Around April of 1991, my husband and I were working in different areas of service in our church which included working with other couples who were going through marital problems. Because of this, my pastor's wife asked me to attend some Bible studies over the next few months that many of these wives needed to attend, thinking that my attendance would encourage them to come. These Kay Arthur Bible studies included her study on *Joy, Lord Heal My Hurts, Lord*

I Need Grace to Make It, and *Marriage without Regrets.* I really didn't see where I needed to go through these studies myself, because I was living the perfect life. I had a husband I could trust who loved me and had blessed me with three wonderful children. We were extremely active in church and were very happy. My husband had just received a big award in his line of business which also included a big promotion. Finally, all the long hours and hard work had paid off. He even spoke of how God had blessed him, because he had been patient and obedient to do God's work and wait on God's timing. This was actually spoken in front of over one hundred people attending a revival service we had gone to at a friend's church.

About three weeks after that proclamation, I felt as if I was having the worst nightmare of my life. It was then that my husband announced to me that "he wasn't happy and he wanted out." My initial reaction was rather calm, because I was so sure of God's presence at that moment. We had been going through a lot of emotional things with other family members having problems, so I just felt like this was Satan attacking us because we were trying to help others. No need to get upset, because I knew God would fix it. After trying to reason with my husband for a couple of hours and seeing no change in his thoughts, I told him I had to go for a drive and try to think through all of this that he had just dumped in my lap. What I was really going to do was go get my brother who lived up the road from us and was my husband's best friend at the time. I just knew he would know what to say and how to snap him out of this kind of thinking. As God would have it, my brother was not home. I drove back toward my house crying uncontrollably, and almost ran off the road. I quickly pulled over on the side of the road to calm down and get myself together before going back to my family. While I was there, I cried out to God in anger and frustration saying, "Why have you let this happen to me and my children?!" Just as clearly as you are reading the written words on this page, God spoke plainly to me when He said, "I haven't let this happen to you and your children... your husband is choosing, on his own free will, to do this. I'm still here, and I'm still God. Now, you're either going to trust Me, or your children will be confused on Who I really am to you and what you've been teaching them about Me. Take My hand and I'll get you through this…I won't leave you…I love you." At that moment, I knew my children's eternity would depend on my response to this terrible situation. I was going to have to go back home, dry my tears, and show them that God is still God even when we don't understand what's going on.

I shared all that with you to let you know that I was truly torn into pieces and didn't know what to do. I was always one to think things through so that everything would always turn out right. Now, I was completely helpless and had to depend on God more than I ever had at any other time in my life.

Had I ever gone through other "tough times?" You bet, I had. My dad left my mother after twenty-six years of marriage after I was grown and married, but that didn't make it hurt any less. I had always tried to be obedient to my parents and had trusted everything my dad taught me, so I was devastated when this happened. However, I knew I still had my husband, so I was going to be okay. My mother became very bitter over the situation and led a fairly unhappy life for years to come. I watched her become very judgmental and critical, and her physical well-being began to go downhill as well. Eventually, she couldn't live on her own and had to come live with me and my three children. Now, as a result of her health problems, she is in a nursing home just waiting for God to take her home. She is completely bed-ridden and has no quality of life.

After going through two years of depression myself, I looked at my mother and decided I didn't want to be bitter like she had been for so many years. I wanted to be happy again. With another man? No...not unless God wanted that for me! I just wanted to be able to laugh genuinely and feel good at the end of a day. The only way I saw how to do that was in forgiving my former husband. Yes, he left and remarried two days after our divorce was final. To top it all off, his new wife quickly became pregnant. I didn't want my children to grow up with any ill feelings toward this innocent little child, so I knew I had to demonstrate forgiveness. Charles Haddon Spurgeon was quoted as saying, "It is very well to rest on God when you have other props, but it is best of all to rest on Him when every prop is knocked away."

Long story short, that precious young lady (almost fifteen, now) is as important to me as my three children. She has blessed my life in so many ways, and has helped keep me true to my claims of being a Christian. My former husband and I get along great now, and his wife and I are close friends. You see, **it is not about me...it's about what others will see in me, and I pray they see Jesus!**

You know, we get so caught-up in this world; we often don't look any different than the rest of the world, or the non-believers, in our response to the "bad things" in our lives. Did I forgive my former husband right away? No. I thought I had, but God quickly showed me that I was only fooling myself. I realized that I was only hurting myself and my children in not truly letting go and letting God handle the whole situation. If you read the Lord's Prayer in Matthew 6: 9-13, you will see that you are asking God to forgive you as you forgive others who do wrong against you! When God revealed that to me, I realized I wasn't forgiving God's way. I was just speaking the forgiveness, not demonstrating it. I was also blocking any blessings God may be wanting to pour out on me and my children, because of my own sin of not truly forgiving. The necessity of forgiveness is spoken in Mark 11:25-26. Read it and you'll see why as a teacher, a mother, and a grandmother now, I tell all my children that talk is cheap and your actions prove what's in your heart.

Do I want someone to miss eternal life because of my lack of forgiveness? Absolutely not! That is what will happen if we can't demonstrate God's love and forgiveness to all and for any reason. Is it hard? Yes! It's a daily commitment to God and wanting others to see Him, rather than getting revenge or making myself feel better. When we truly realize that we give up ALL "rights" when we give our lives to God and promise to live for Him, then lives will be changed. Lip service lasts about as long as it takes to get the words out of your mouth, but a demonstration is like an image that is burned into our minds forever! Do you really want to be remembered as being one of the most Godly people your friends and family members have ever known? Start with forgiveness.

Whether others receive it, or not, will not matter…It's the attitude of your heart and your desire to be more like Christ. You can only change your ways, and leave the rest to God. I pray God can help you see the value of forgiveness. Follow Colossians 3:12–13 where He says, "Therefore, as the elect of God, holy and beloved, put on tender mercies, kindness, humility, meekness, longsuffering; bearing with one another, and forgiving one another, if anyone has a complaint against another; even as Christ forgave you, so you also must do."

God wants to use our suffering to make us better, not bitter. Think about your life and the things you are going through. Have you been able to forgive, or are you still holding on to your pain?

CHAPTER 12
WHO DO I TALK TO?

Who does God want us to talk to, and what does God want us to say when someone else is mistreating us, hurting us, and causing us to suffer? Psalms gives us many examples of David talking to God about those who hurt him and caused him to suffer. David is very honest as he cries out to God about his hurts and about how horrible the people are who hurt him. In Psalm 142, David tells God all of his complaints and troubles:

- I am overwhelmed by the situation
- Men have hidden a snare for me
- No one is concerned for me
- I have no refuge
- No one cares
- I am in desperate need

- I need rescue from those who are pursuing me
- My enemy is too strong for me
- I am in a prison

David shows us that we need to take our cares to God, cry to Him, and tell Him EVERYTHING that is happening to us. I love to read the Psalms when I am hurting, because I see myself and my pain. I see how much God cares and how God is my refuge, my ever present help in time of trouble. I know God wants us to bring all of our burdens, cares, problems, and concerns to Him. Often we just think about our problems and continue to think of ways to solve them; our minds are consumed with the thoughts. We just keep going around and around like a merry-go-round. We try to solve our problems over and over in our minds. But if we are just talking to ourselves, we are not praying and taking our problems before our Lord. God knows our every thought, but OUR THOUGHTS ARE NOT PRAYERS. When you are talking to yourself you are thinking, but when you are talking to God you are praying. God wants us to pray. He wants us to tell Him our hurts and our needs. He wants us to ask Him for wisdom.

Pray, pour it all out before God, and then you can start thanking Him for His answers. *Thinking* wears you out, but *thanking* Him brings His strength. Being grateful opens the door for God to begin His work on your behalf, and it gives you a lighter, more peaceful feeling, because it helps you focus on God's love for you. It is truly something to be thankful for when you realize that you have Almighty God working on your behalf.

Prayer is so powerful, and a prayer partner or a prayer group is one of the greatest blessings you can have. I am so privileged to have my mother and sisters as my prayer partners. We pray for each other about everything. All of my mother's grandchildren tease each other about being on our prayer list, but they have learned that God answers prayer, and they know where to turn for help. If you don't already have a prayer partner, ask God to lead you to a person or a group. You need their support, and they need yours.

Pastors' wives know that they seldom have anyone to talk to. But that may be a blessing in disguise, because it makes us turn to God, the only one who has all the answers. And no matter what we tell Him, He doesn't need to gossip and tell our hurts. He'll still love us and our loved ones, and He doesn't take sides. He only comforts us, gives us strength, fills us with hope, protects us, blesses us, and works everything out for our good and for His glory.

Sometimes we need to talk to another person. I love to be there for women who have problems. I feel God wants me to encourage them to turn to Him and solve the problem His way. I want to help them embrace the suffering as a friend, and learn what God wants to lovingly teach them.

DON'T WRESTLE, JUST NESTLE

Corrie ten Boom, who was a prisoner of war and saw her whole family tortured and killed, says, "Don't wrestle; just nestle." This is not easy, because it is our nature to wrestle. When you learn to nestle in the arms of God, and talk to him like David did, your wrestling can cease. In the middle of her years as a prisoner, she kept reminding herself, "This, too, shall pass." I have said that to comfort myself many times, especially when my children were growing up.

It is easy to see that the arms of God are so much better than my continued frustration and fighting to get my way. We will all suffer, but our suffering is for nothing unless we stop focusing on our circumstances, and instead focus on God and what He is doing. This is how we rise above our circumstances and get free of the burdens we are carrying.

When you really must talk to another person, be very careful who you talk to. Pray and ask God to show you the right person for you. He cares, and He will show you the one who will point you to Him. Sometimes our friends are not the best people to talk to, because they love us and they do not want to see us suffer. They may tell us what they know we want to hear rather than what we need to hear.

If you are having problems in your marriage, be very careful about talking to a man. Spend much time in prayer asking God to lead you to the man or woman He knows will be best for you. Think about it, maybe there is a man at work who listens to you, and your husband does not. You are leaving the door wide open for Satan if you allow another man to meet your needs when you think your husband is not there for you and not meeting your needs. Having a close relationship with another man can/will make your suffering much worse, and you will end up causing a lot more people to suffer. You've seen it happen many times, and so have I.

Whatever your problem, remember that God knows the right answer and who will be the best person to help you. He is not going to send you to someone who will tell you things that make the problem go on and on, and get even worse. He is going to send you to a person who will speak the truth in love and help you see God's plan and His purpose. He is going to send you to a person who will listen to you, but not allow you to stay in the pit. It will be a person who helps you remember who God is and see the big picture. Sometimes it is good to share your burden with another person, because we need the love, support, prayer, and encouragement.

What would happen when you get to heaven, if God asks you why you responded the way you did in a certain trial or suffering? The right answer would NOT be: "I couldn't do anything you wanted me to do, Lord, because it was my husband's, my boss's, my parents', or someone else's fault." Your trial may be someone else's fault, but are you responding like Jesus would? You are not responsible for anyone else's actions toward you; you are only responsible for your response. You may need someone to help you see the steps you should take to be pleasing to God. HE WANTS TO KNOW WHAT <u>YOU</u> DID, NOT WHAT THEY DID. God will take that up with them.

You must not waste your time talking about your problem to someone who allows you to go over the situation again and again. He/she is only allowing you to waste your time and energy. It will make you tired and frustrated. Going over your pain aloud or in your mind will wear you out. You must ask God to help you find someone who will encourage you to focus on the big picture and look at the problem from God's perspective. Then you can respond to the problem the way God would have you to.

These verses will help you know what to say whether you are the counselor or the counselee.

Take control of what I say, O Lord,
and keep my lips sealed.
— *Psalm 141:3 NLT*

*Stop judging others and you will not
be judged. Stop criticizing others, or
it will all come back on you. If you
forgive others, you will be forgiven.*

— *Luke 6:37 NLT*

*Don't use foul or abusive language.
Let everything you say be good and
helpful, so that your words will be an
encouragement to those who hear them.*

— *Ephesians 4:29 NLT*

*Kindness is the rule for everything
she says.*

— *Proverbs 31:26 The Living Bible*

*When words are many, sin is not
absent, but he who holds his tongue
is wise.*

— *Proverbs 10:19 NIV*

CHAPTER 13
GIVE THANKS

Give thanks in all circumstances; for this is the will of God in Christ Jesus for you.

— *I Thessalonians 5:18 ESV*

Consider it pure joy when you encounter various trials.

— *James 1:2-4 NIV*

Therefore, we do not lose heart...For our light and momentary troubles are achieving for us an eternal glory that far outweighs them all. So we fix our eyes not on what is seen, but on what is unseen. For what is seen is temporary, but what is unseen is eternal.

— *2 Corinthians 4:16-18 NIV*

We can rejoice, too, when we run into problems and trials, for we know that they are good for us – they help us learn to endure. And endurance develops strength of character in us, and character strengthens our confident expectation of salvation. And this expectation will not disappoint us. For we know how dearly God loves us, because He has given us the Holy Spirit to fill our hearts with love.
— *Romans 5:3-8 NLT*

Since God says to give thanks in everything, then there must be something good in everything that happens to me. The verses above in both James and Romans say that our trials develop our faith, produce endurance, and make us strong in character and ready for anything. Those things are good, and I can give thanks for the fact that the mess I am in is making me strong in character and ready for anything.

The verses in 2 Corinthians at the beginning of this chapter tell us that our troubles are light and momentary when compared to the glory of eternity that is so heavy (so wonderful) that it outweighs the suffering in our lives. Our suffering is momentary when compared with eternity, and

there is no suffering in eternity. So we must fix our eyes on Christ, the unseen, and not on the suffering we see. We must focus on Jesus, God, the eternal.

We can give thanks, because we can see how God is using our sufferings to make us better, to strengthen our character, to make us more like Jesus, and to let us be an example to the hurting world. We can give thanks, because we see the big picture, we know that God is our portion, and we know that God is doing what pleases Him and what is best for us.

Think on these things:

> *Whatever is true, whatever is right, whatever is pure, whatever is lovely, whatever is admirable — if anything is excellent or praiseworthy — think about such things.*
> *— Philippians 4:8 NIV*

God wants us to think about the positive things. It is a proven fact that people who are positive live longer than those who are negative. I believe that Jesus was positive, and He means for us to be positive. The Bible is a very positive book, even in the midst of strife, struggles, and sin.

TEACH YOUR CHILDREN

Do everything you can to teach your children and grandchildren how to be victorious in the unpleasant things that happen to them. Your example is their best teacher. When something happens that causes you or your child to suffer, what do you do? Do you become a victim or victorious? Your response is so important. If you have a good attitude, and respond to the situation and the person causing it as Jesus asks you to, you are teaching your child to be victorious.

If you respond with anger, threats, retaliation, pouting, or in any other hurtful way, you are teaching your child to be a victim.

Teachers are a necessary part of a child's life. If the teacher loves your child and has the same basic personality as your child, life is wonderful. But our children had a few "mean" teachers, and I'm sure that your children will, too. These teachers are not necessarily mean, but they do things a different way, and may not appreciate all the "cute" things your child does. Please ask God to help you use this negative situation for good in your child's life. Try to see the strengths in the teacher and ask God to work these strengths into your child's life. Ask the teacher what you can do to help your child be successful in his class, and then work with your child to accomplish this. Pray for the teacher.

If you agree that the teacher is mean, side with your child, try to get a different teacher, you may be limiting the character development of your child. Since God is in control of your child's life, you need to find out what God may be trying to teach your child with this teacher, and help your child cooperate with the teacher.

I want to teach my two granddaughters to be positive. Once we were on a walk and we found a beautiful butterfly wing. At first they were very sad for the butterfly, because it could not fly with only one wing.

I didn't want them to focus on the bad, so I asked, "What can the one winged butterfly do?"

"It can walk," they said together.

Then we talked about how the butterfly was still alive, it could walk around, and it could talk to its friends. We were looking for the good.

How are you like the butterfly with only one wing? What is missing in your life? A husband? Children? Job? Your hearing? Your ability to walk? Have you lost a breast due to cancer? Are you lonely? **How are you dealing with what is missing in your life?**

I want you to look for the good. It can become a game that you play with your children and grandchildren. It can become a habit. It can be a way you help your friends when they come to you for help with their problems.

Those who see the good in their lives, even in the painful things that happen to them, see things to be thankful for. Those who only look at the bad have a sad life. There is something good in every bad thing that happens to us, as Christians. Romans 8:28 says, *"All things work together for good."* Sometimes we have to look for the good. When we cannot see it, we can still know that God is doing as He says and working good in our life, especially in our character, as He makes us more like Him.

Think about this example: A father grew sick and lost his job; he was devastated. He had been working so hard that he had not really been a part of his family for years. His children had become spoiled, his wife was considering divorce, and he didn't even know his family. As the weeks went by, and the wife had to work to take care of the family, the children had to be home with Dad to help take care of him. Dad decided to make the best of this terrible situation, so he began to do what he could to grow closer to his family. In time, the children had the father they needed. Since he was home all the time, he began to see what life had been like for his wife. He began to appreciate her, not only for what she had done in the past, but for what she was doing to provide for the family. She began to see and feel some of the pressure he had been going through to provide all the things the family wanted and needed. Amazingly, they began to appreciate each other, and as Dad healed and they got to know each other again, their family healed, too. Do you see the good that came from that trial and suffering? Of course, you do.

As trials continually come into our lives, I pray that we will look to God and ask Him to help us see the bright side and the good that can and will come if we trust in Him, and let Him have His way in our lives.

CHAPTER 14
THE BRIGHT SIDE OF DARKNESS

I want you to read this article written by my sister. It is the most inspiring summary of physical suffering I have ever seen. As you read it, I pray that God will speak to you and help you see the bright side of your suffering.

> The word suffering brings to mind a lot of scary thoughts: Cancer, Death, Accidents, Tears, Pain, Loneliness, or Hospitals. But what I have experienced in these months of suffering has not been terrible. In fact, if I could choose to do this over I would not choose health. I am not saying that I like pain, inactivity, or the inconvenience to my family and friends. But I am saying that this time of "suffering" has been wonderful in many ways.

First of all, I am confident of God's unfailing love for me because, "The Lord disciplines those He loves," (Proverbs 3:12). Webster defines discipline this way: "Training which corrects, molds, or perfects the mental faculties or moral character." So I see this suffering not as a punishment but as a gift. This gift, when unwrapped, contains things I never would have experienced any other way.

Another thing that I am learning is that all suffering produces some benefit. Yes, even suffering as a result of unwise choices or disobedience. The reason I can say with confidence that all suffering produces some benefit is because God is good. And because He is good, and because He loves us with a love we cannot understand, He has promised in His Word that our suffering will develop character in our lives. Romans 5:3-5 says, "Not only so, but we also rejoice in our sufferings, because we know that suffering produces perseverance; perseverance character, and character, hope. And hope does not disappoint us, because God has poured out His love into our hearts by the Holy Spirit, whom He has given us."

God says suffering produces perseverance. He doesn't say suffering may produce perseverance. Nor does He say suffering could produce perseverance if you respond correctly. He says suffering produces perseverance! That sounds to me like that is a job that only God can do in my life. And if God wants to produce perseverance, which develops character, which gives hope, then He must first allow me to suffer.

Can a lump of clay become a beautiful, functional pitcher without first being pounded and pushed, spun and heated? Can gold become pure, brilliant and lovely without first experiencing the heat of the fire? Can the blacksmith make anything of use without first placing his iron in the fire and then striking this iron with great force time after time?

The same is true for us as Christians. If we desire to know Him and be used by Him, He must first mold us. He continues throughout our life to mold and shape us according to the plan He established for us before we were born (Psalms 139:16). Because of His great love, He is committed to the process of completing the work He began in me (Philippians 1:6).

So, I have learned through suffering that God loves me extravagantly and that He wants me to benefit from this suffering.

However, I am also seeing that not only will I benefit, but those around me benefit as well; because if I suffer, they suffer. And if they suffer God promises to produce Godly character in them beginning with perseverance.

Many times I feel guilty because I know that my suffering is causing my family to suffer. They suffer in many ways. They don't like to see me in pain and it makes them angry. It puts added burdens and responsibilities on them, because they have to take up the slack. When I am completely helpless I feel like I am such a burden to them. They feel frustrated because they want to help and don't know what to do. They want this problem to be over so that life can get back to "normal" (whatever that is!). So I feel guilty that because of my suffering, many suffer. But, I have to remember, God is Good, and He wants to bless them in their suffering.

Another thing I am learning, but I need to remember this especially when I am feeling guilty, God is sovereign and His plans for me are good. Jeremiah 29:11 says, "For I know the plans I have for you, declares the Lord, Plans to prosper you and not to harm you, plans to give you hope and a future." And His plans for me are designed to bring Him glory. He has His own purpose in this for His own sake.

Isaiah 48:10-11, "See, I have refined you, though not as silver; I have tested you in the furnace of affliction. For my own sake, for my own sake, I do this." How can my affliction be for His own sake? Of what benefit can my suffering be to the Father? I am only a little speck in the grand scheme of things; a flower that flourishes today and is gone tomorrow. I would hope that the work of God might be displayed in my life whether in sickness or in health. John 9:3 says of the man born blind, "Neither has this man nor his parents sinned," said Jesus, "but this happened so that the work of God might be displayed in his life." I am confident that God is working in my life for my good. But I also hope that this would be of some benefit to others and bring glory to God.

CHAPTER 15
SAFE IN THE HOLLOW
OF HIS HAND

Walking through this world of darkness,
Never knowing what you'll face.
Tears and fears are all around us,
As are moments of disgrace.
Jesus said that He'd be with me
and would hold me tenderly,
That I'd be safe in the hollow of
His Hand.

There are times I feel unable
Just to handle all my cares.
And the load seems, Oh, so heavy
there are tears in all my prayers.
But I know that He has promised to help
me always stand,
And I am safe in the hollow of His hands.

Then one day I'll hear the angels
as they gently call me home.
And I'll have to leave my loved ones,
Far behind here, all alone
As I step into the Jordan,
I know I'll get to Beulah Land,
For I am safe in the hollow of His hands.

Chorus
I am safe in the hollow of His hand.
I am safe in the hollow of His hand .
Though all Hell may come against me
And I feel I cannot stand,
I am safe in the hollow of His hand.

Words and Music By Eddie West
1997

This song says it all. No matter what happens in the darkness of our sufferings, we are safe in the Hollow of His Hands. Our worlds and our lives are brightened over and over when we run to the safety of His Hands.

IN CLOSING…

Thank you for reading this book. I pray that you have been blessed with inspiration and information to help you climb out of your darkness into God's brightness.

This book is a miracle, and I must tell you why. In the past years, I had tried to write several different books for women or for Pastors' wives, because I love helping women be the best they can be for God. Every time I tried, it seemed to be too difficult, and I would quit.

About a month ago, we had an exciting experience with a Pastor and his wife from a small church. When I told my mother, she said that I should write the story, but as I made excuses and tried to say, "No," she asked me to just pray about it. I did pray about it, and I told God that I would do anything He wanted me to do. I yielded myself totally to Him, and forgot about writing; I just prayed sincerely for God to use me any way He desired.

Three weeks ago, I felt God was telling me it was His time for me to write a book. I was excited and told Eddie that God wanted me to write a book for the conference we were going to have in September. It is planned for Pastors of small churches, and their wives are invited. I was thrilled that I would have a book to use with the wives. Eddie was excited, too, and told me that I had better call Jeff, our brother-in-law, to see about publishing deadlines.

Jeff said it was not possible to get a book written and published by September. I agreed, but told him God said to do it, so I knew God would make it happen. He told me that my part of the book had to be completed in three weeks.

I began the book, thinking I was writing to Pastors' wives, but as God revealed His plan, I was suddenly writing a book on suffering. God is good. He poured out the book, and provided people to proofread, edit, and critique. He totally worked everything out, and here is the book…in exactly three weeks!! I am not a writer, but with God in me, all things are possible. I thank Him and praise Him for His amazing goodness.

I pray that this book will help you in the days to come and that all of us will accept our sufferings as friends, and let God use them to teach us His truths.

ABOUT THE AUTHOR

Glenda West is a Pastor's wife, a mother, and a grandmother. She is a retired school teacher who loved teaching. She is working with her husband Eddie in a ministry to pastors of small churches. They are committed to keeping pastors in the ministry. She and her husband of forty years live in North Augusta, South Carolina.

ORDERING AND CONTACT INFORMATION

You can order additional copies of *The Bright Side of Darkness* through:

www.ledgepress.com

www.amazon.com

www.upsidedownministries.com

If you have an idea or a dream of writing and publishing your own book then check out the possibilities at www.ledgepress.com.

Or write:

L'Edge Press

PO Box 2567

Boone, NC 28607

Printed in the United States
187LV00001BB/1-246/A

9 780976 201489